The Caterpillar Story

EDUCATIONAL AND READING CONSULTANTS

Diana Bentley and Dee Reid, Senior Lecturers in Language and Reading,
Oxford Brookes University

Published by Evans Brothers Limited
2A Portman Mansions
Chiltern Street
London, W1U 6NR

First published in this edition 2005

Printed in China by W K T Co., Ltd.

ISBN 0 237 52916 5

ACKNOWLEDGEMENTS
Planning and production by Discovery Books
Design by Simon Balley Design Associates
Picture research by Helena Ramsay
Edited by Kate Johnson
Typesetting by Graphic Action

For permission to reproduce copyright material, the author and publishers
gratefully acknowledge the following:
Heather Angel: cover (top left), page 7, 11; NHPA: cover (bottom) and page 28;
Natural Science Photos: (D. Meredith) pages 17, 19, 21, 25, (T.A. Moss A.R.P.S.) pages 15, 27,
(P.H. & S.L. Ward) page 23, (Andrew Watts) pages 13, 21.

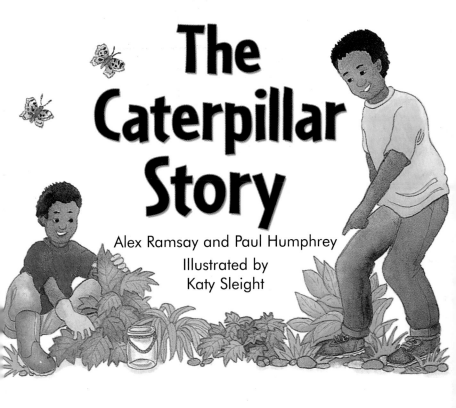

The Caterpillar Story

Alex Ramsay and Paul Humphrey

Illustrated by
Katy Sleight

Evans

5

6

They are young caterpillars.

Yes, but you must look after it
properly.

9

I'll bring in some of the leaves you found it on.

11

12

They help it to cling on to
the plants it eats.

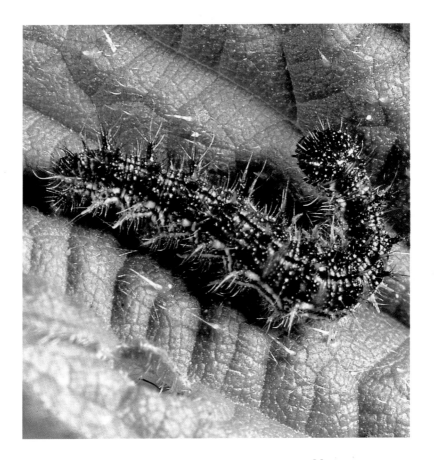

As it grows, a caterpillar
changes its skin.

16

He's eaten a lot of leaves.

18

He has started to change. Just wait and see.

19

 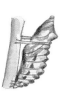

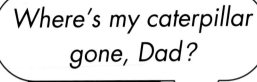

20

It has turned into a chrysalis.
What happens next is very
exciting.

And look what's coming out.

23

Yes, and now it's drying its wings in the sunshine.

26

It's ready to fly away now.
Open the window.

27

It's going out to find some flowers. Soon it will lay eggs and what will come out of the eggs?

More caterpillars!

29

Here are the stages in the caterpillar story. How many of them can you remember?

Index